Janice VanCleave's
WILD, WACKY, AND WEIRD
Science Experiments

Even More of Janice VanCleave's
Wild, Wacky, and Weird
ASTRONOMY
EXPERIMENTS

Illustrations by
Jim Carroll

rosen publishing's
rosen
central

This edition published in 2018 by The Rosen Publishing Group, Inc.
29 East 21st Street
New York, NY 10010

Library of Congress Cataloging-in-Publication Data

Names: VanCleave, Janice Pratt.
Title: Even more of Janice VanCleave's wild, wacky, and weird astronomy experiments / Janice VanCleave.
Other titles: Janice VanCleave's wild, wacky, and weird astronomy experiments
Description: New York : Rosen Publishing, 2018. | Series: Janice VanCleave's wild, wacky, and weird science experiments | Audience: Grades 5–8. | Includes bibliographical references and index.
Identifiers: LCCN 2016053659| ISBN 9781499466911 (pbk. book) | ISBN 9781499466782 (6 pack) | ISBN 9781499466867 (library bound book)
Subjects: LCSH: Astronomy—Experiments—Juvenile literature.
Classification: LCC QB46 .V3638 2018 | DDC 520.078—dc23
LC record available at https://lccn.loc.gov/2016053659

Manufactured in China

Illustrations by Jim Carroll

Experiments first published in *Janice VanCleave's 200 Gooey, Slippery, Slimy, Weird and Fun Experiments* by John Wiley & Sons, Inc. copyright © 1992 Janice VanCleave

CONTENTS

INTRODUCTION

For as long as humans have existed, they have looked to the heavens in an attempt to understand the stars, the planets, and our sun. In modern times, we have rocketed into space to land on the moon. We have built the International Space Station to do research in space and powerful telescopes to peer at the far reaches of the universe. Perhaps humans will someday visit Mars.

Astronomy is the study of the planets, the stars, and other bodies in space. The people who decide to work in the field of astronomy have a variety of career paths to choose from. Some scientists study the planets and others study galaxies. Some astronomers work to learn more about black holes and the universe. Solar scientists focus on our sun, the star that enables life to exist on Earth. All of these people have something in common: they are constantly asking questions to learn even more about space.

This book is a collection of science experiments about astronomy. Why does the moon stay in orbit? How do satellites work? How does gravity affect the movement of celestial bodies? You will find the answers to these and many other questions by doing the experiments in this book.

HOW TO USE THIS BOOK

You will be rewarded with successful experiments if you read each experiment carefully, follow the steps in order, and do not substitute materials. The following sections are included for all the experiments.

» **PURPOSE:** *The basic goals for the experiment.*

» **MATERIALS:** *A list of supplies you will need.* You will experience less frustration and more fun if you gather all the necessary materials for the experiments before you begin. You lose your train of thought when you have to stop and search for supplies.

» **PROCEDURE:** *Step-by-step instructions on how to perform the experiment.* Follow each step very carefully, never skip steps, and do not add your own. Safety is of the utmost importance, and by reading the experiment before starting, then following the instructions exactly, you can feel confident that no unexpected results will occur. Ask an adult to help you when you are working with anything sharp or hot. If adult supervision is required, it will be noted in the experiment.

» **RESULTS:** *An explanation stating exactly what is expected to happen.* This is an immediate learning tool. If the expected results are achieved, you will know that you did the experiment correctly. If your results are not the same as described in the experiment, carefully read the instructions and start over from the first step.

» **WHY?** *An explanation of why the results were achieved.*

INTRODUCTION

THE SCIENTIFIC METHOD

Scientists identify a problem or observe an event. Then they seek solutions or explanations through research and experimentation. By doing the experiments in this book, you will learn to follow experimental steps and make observations. You will also learn many scientific principles that have to do with astronomy.

In the process, the things you see or learn may lead you to new questions. For example, perhaps you have completed the experiment that uses a mirror to demonstrate how satellites work. Now you wonder what would happen if you changed the angle of the mirror. That's great! All scientists are curious and ask new questions about what they learn. When you design a new experiment, it is a good idea to follow the scientific method.

1. Ask a question.

2. Do some research about your question. What do you already know?

3. Come up with a hypothesis, or a possible answer to your question.

4. Design an experiment to test your hypothesis. Make sure the experiment is repeatable.

5. Collect the data and make observations.

6. Analyze your results.

7. Reach a conclusion. Did your results support your hypothesis?

Many times the experiment leads to more questions and a new experiment.

Always remember that when devising your own science experiment, have a knowledgeable adult review it with you before trying it out. Ask them to supervise it as well.

ELLIPTICAL

PURPOSE To determine how gravity affects the movement of celestial bodies.

MATERIALS 1 sheet of printer paper
1 sheet of carbon paper
clipboard
modeling clay
cardboard tube from paper towel roll
large glass marble

PROCEDURE

1. Place the printer paper on the clipboard.

2. Lay the carbon paper on top of the printer paper, carbon side down.

3. Place both sheets under the clip on the board.

4. Raise the clip end of the board by placing two marble-sized balls of clay under both corners.

5. Place one end of the cardboard tube on top of the papers.

6. The tube should be parallel with the top of the clipboard.

7. Slightly elevate the tube by placing a ball of clay under one end.

8. Place the marble in the elevated end of the tube and allow it to roll out of the tube and across the papers.

9. Raise the carbon sheet and observe the pattern produced on the printer paper.

RESULTS The pattern made by the marble is curved. *Note:* Increase the elevation of the clipboard if the marble's path is not curved.

WHY? The marble has a horizontal speed and would continue to move straight across the paper if gravity did not pull it downward. The forward force plus the downward pull moves the marble in a curved path. The paths of planets are also affected by the gravitational pull of the sun. All the planets have forward motions as well as a pull toward the sun. If the sun had no gravitational attraction, the planets would not orbit the sun but would move away from the sun in a straight line.

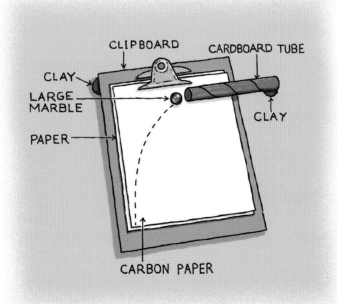

CLIPBOARD · CARDBOARD TUBE · CLAY · LARGE MARBLE · CLAY · PAPER · CARBON PAPER

SATELLITE CRASH

PURPOSE To demonstrate why a satellite stays in orbit.

MATERIALS poster board   large, empty, 3-lb. (1.4-kg) coffee can
            pencil   masking tape
            ruler   glass marble
            scissors

PROCEDURE

1. On the poster board, draw a circle with a 22 in. (55 cm) diameter.

2. Cut around the circle, then cut out a wedge (pie slice) that is one-eighth of the circle.

3. Overlap the circle to form a cone that fits snugly in the coffee can with most of the cone sticking out the top of the can. Tape the cone so it does not open up.

4. Tape the cone to the outside of the can.

5. Roll the marble around the top of the cone as fast as possible and observe its movement.

RESULTS The marble rolls around the inside of the cone, and its path begins to curve downward as the speed of the marble slows. The marble finally moves to the bottom of the cone and stops.

WHY? The paper offers a continuous resistance to the movement of the marble, forcing it to move in a circular path, and gravity pulls the marble downward. As the forward speed of the marble decreases, the unchanging pull of gravity forces the marble to move down the cone toward the bottom.

Satellites would continue to circle Earth if they never lost their forward motion, but like the marble, as their speed decreases, gravity pulls them toward Earth until finally they crash into Earth. Planets and moons are examples of satellites since they all orbit another celestial body; they would crash if their forward speed decreased.

ORBITER

PURPOSE To demonstrate the force that keeps satellites in orbit around Earth.

MATERIALS small-mouthed glass jar, 1 pint (500 ml)
glass marble

PROCEDURE

1. Use your hand to hold the jar horizontally with its opening pointing to the side.

2. Place a marble inside the jar.

3. Gently place the mouth of the jar against the palm of your other hand.

4. Move the jar around in a circular path until the marble quickly spins around on the inside of the jar.

5. Continue to move the jar around as you slowly turn the jar and your palm upside down. You may have to practice this movement to keep the marble moving at a constant speed.

6. Remove your palm from the mouth of the jar.

7. Stop moving the jar.

RESULTS The marble remains inside the jar as long as the jar is spun. The marble continues to spin for a short time after you stop moving the jar, but finally the marble slows and falls out of the jar.

WHY? The jar pushes on the marble and provides an inward force that keeps the marble moving in a circular path. This force toward the center is called a centripetal force. The word centripetal means "seeking the center." If the bottle were suddenly removed, the marble would fly off in a straight line because of its forward speed. Any object moving in a circular path—the marble, a moon, or an artificial satellite—has a forward speed and a centripetal force pulling it inward. Earth's natural and artificial satellites are pulled toward Earth's surface by gravity, but their own forward speed keeps them from being pulled into Earth. Satellites, like the marble, fall when their forward speed decreases.

SHUT OUT

PURPOSE To demonstrate the effect of a lunar eclipse on studying the sun's corona.

MATERIALS index card
straight pin
desk lamp

PROCEDURE

Caution: NEVER look at the sun directly because it can damage your eyes.

1. Use the straight pin to make a hole in the center of the card.

2. Slightly hollow out the hole so that you can see through it.

3. Turn the lamp on.

4. Close your right eye.

5. Hold the card in front of your left eye.

6. Look through the pinhole at the bulb of the glowing lamp.

RESULTS The print on the outside of the bulb can be read when looking through the pinhole.

WHY? The card shuts out most of the light from the bulb, allowing the print to be visible. During a solar eclipse, the moon blocks the glaring light from the sun, allowing the less intense glowing outer surface, or corona, to be studied.

TRAPPED

PURPOSE To determine how Earth is protected from solar winds.

MATERIALS bar magnet
2 sheets of notebook paper
iron filings (available online or at some teacher/office supply stores)
drinking straw

PROCEDURE

1. Cover the magnet with one sheet of paper.

2. Fold the second sheet of paper and sprinkle iron filings in the fold.

3. Hold the paper about 6 in. (15 cm) from the magnet.

4. Blow through the straw.

5. Direct the stream of air at the iron filings in the folded paper. A stream of iron filings are blown toward the magnet.

RESULTS Particles of iron stick to the paper in the shape of the underlying magnet.

WHY? Around the magnet is a magnetic force field that attracts the iron filings. Earth has a magnetic force field surrounding it. The area affected by the magnetic field is called the magnetosphere. The magnetosphere deflects and traps charged particles from the sun, much as the magnet under the paper attracted the iron filings. The charged particles come from the sun as a result of solar flares and sunspots. These moving particles are called solar winds and reach Earth's orbit at speeds up to 1 to 2 million miles/hr (1.6 to 3.2 million km/hr). Astronauts in space could be in danger from solar flare particles because the high-energy particles damage living tissue. Without Earth's magnetosphere, living organisms on Earth would be in danger from the charged particles.

RISER

PURPOSE To determine how the sun can be seen before it rises above the horizon.

MATERIALS 1 clear glass jar with a lid, 1 qt. (1 liter)
table
books
ruler
modeling clay

PROCEDURE

1. Fill the jar to overflowing with water.

2. Tightly screw the lid on the jar.

3. Lay the jar on its side on a table about 12 in. (30 cm) from the edge of the table.

4. On the edge of the table in front of the jar, stack books so that about one-fourth of the jar rises above the books.

5. Make a ball of clay about the size of a walnut.

6. Lay the clay ball on the table about 4 in. (10 cm) from the jar.

7. Kneel down in front of the books.

8. Look straight across the top surface of the books and through the jar of water. If the clay ball is not visible, move it to a new position.

9. Keeping your head in this position, move the jar out of your line of vision.

RESULTS You can see the clay ball only by looking through the jar of water.

WHY? Looking through the jar of water allows you to see the clay ball even though it is below the level of the top of the books. Everything you look at is seen because light from that object reaches your eye. The light from the clay ball passed through the jar and was refracted (bent) toward your eye. Light from objects in the sky passes through Earth's atmosphere (hundreds of miles of air surrounding Earth) before reaching your eyes. Earth's atmosphere causes light to be refracted in the same way as does the jar of water. Because of the refraction of light, you see the sun a few minutes before it actually rises above the horizon in the morning and for a few minutes after it sets in the afternoon.

BRIGHT SPOT

PURPOSE To safely observe the image of the sun.

MATERIALS

1 large box—the author used a box
   12 in. x 12 in. x 24 in. (30 cm x 30 cm
   x 60 cm)
scissors
binoculars

index card
masking tape
aluminum foil
1 sheet of printer paper

PROCEDURE

Caution: NEVER look at the sun through binoculars because it will damage your eyes. NEVER look directly at the sun.

1. Turn the box so that its opening is facing to the side.

2. Cut a hole in the top side of the box just large enough for the small ends of the binoculars to fit into.

3. Cut out a circle from an index card. Tape the paper circle over one of the large ends of the binoculars.

4. Fit the binoculars into the space cut in the top of the box with the small ends down. Secure with tape.

5. Wrap pieces of aluminum foil around the binoculars to seal any open spaces between the binoculars and the box.

6. Set the box outside in a sunny area and sit in front of the open side.

7. Tilt the box so that the open lens of the binoculars points toward the sun and no shadow of the binoculars falls on top of the box. DO NOT

LOOK THROUGH THE BINOCULARS and DO NOT LOOK DIRECTLY AT THE SUN. Look only at the paper in the next step.

8. Hold a sheet of printer paper inside the box, and while looking at the paper, move the paper up and down until the image of the sun is clearly seen on the paper.

RESULTS A bright circle of light is seen on the paper.

WHY? The sun's brilliant light can permanently damage your eyes, so a special instrument must be used to see the image of the sun's surface and not the actual surface. The open lens in the binoculars focuses the light from the sun onto the paper screen, and thus the sun's image can be safely observed.

PACKED

PURPOSE To demonstrate why the sun's center has a greater density (mass of a specific volume) than the outside.

MATERIALS 1 bag miniature marshmallows, 1 lb. (454 g)
plastic cup, 16 oz. (480 ml)
food scale

PROCEDURE

1. Drop marshmallows into a plastic cup one at a time until the marshmallows are even with the top of the cup.

2. Use a food scale to measure the weight of the cup of marshmallows.

3. Remove the cup from the scale and place it on a table.

4. With your fingers, push the marshmallows in the cup down into the cup.

5. Refill the empty space in the cup with marshmallows and again push the marshmallows down to make room for more.

6. Continue to add and press the marshmallows down until no more can be added and the marshmallows are even with the top of the cup.

7. Use the food scale again to measure the weight of the cup.

RESULTS The cup with the pressed marshmallows weighs more.

WHY? The cup has a constant volume (space occupied by matter) and is filled each time with the same material, marshmallows. The cup and its content of marshmallows weigh more when more marshmallows are

Even More of Janice VanCleave's Wild, Wacky, and Weird Astronomy Experiments

pressed into the cup. This experiment demonstrates why the core (center) of the sun has a greater density than the outside. Density is the scientific way of comparing the "heaviness" of materials; it is a measurement of the mass (weight) of a specific volume. The sun is believed to be made of the same material throughout, but samples of the same volume would weigh more if taken near the sun's center. The sun's gravity (pull toward the center) is very great, so the materials near the core are pressed together; therefore the density is greater.

MINIATURE
MARSHMALLOWS

PACKED
IN CUP

FLAMING COLORS

PURPOSE To determine the colors that make up white light from the sun.

MATERIALS shallow baking pan
flat pocket mirror
1 sheet printer paper

PROCEDURE

Caution: This experiment must be done on a sunny day, and you must not look directly at the sun or use the mirror to reflect the sun's light toward another person's eyes.

1. Fill a shallow baking pan with water.

2. Place the pan on a table near a window so that it receives the morning sunlight.

3. Place a flat mirror inside the pan so that it rests at an angle against one side of the pan.

4. With one hand, hold a sheet of white paper in front of the mirror.

5. Use your other hand to move the mirror slightly. Adjust the position of the mirror and paper until a rainbow of colors appears on the white paper.

6. Slightly shake the mirror.

RESULTS Flickering rainbow-colored flames appear on the white paper.

WHY? The layer of water between the mirror and the surface of the water acts like a prism. A prism is a triangular piece of glass that bends the rays of light passing through it so that the light breaks into its separate colors, called a spectrum. The white light of the sun can be separated by a prism into a spectrum of seven colors always appearing in the same order: red, orange, yellow, green, blue, indigo, and violet. The moving water changes the direction of the light, causing the colors to appear like flickering flames.

MIRROR

NIGHT LIGHTS

PURPOSE To simulate and describe the attraction of charged particles near Earth's poles.

MATERIALS paper hole punch
tissue paper
table
round balloon, small enough to hold in your hand
  when inflated
your own hair—be sure it is clean, dry, and oil-free

PROCEDURE

1. Punch twenty to thirty holes out of the tissue paper with the hole punch.

2. Place the paper circles on a table.

3. Stroke the balloon against your hair ten times.

4. Hold the stroked side of the balloon near, but not touching, the paper circles.

RESULTS The paper circles jump toward the balloon. Some of the circles leap off the balloon.

WHY? The paper circles represent charged particles circling Earth at great distances, and the balloon represents Earth. As was explained in Experiment 5, Earth has a magnetosphere around it that deflects and traps charged particles from the sun. The poles of Earth act like strong magnets and pull some of the charged particles from the magnetosphere toward Earth. Unlike the paper circles, the charged

26

particles do not hit and leap from Earth's surface but move around in the upper atmosphere near the poles, bumping into the atoms of gas in the atmosphere. The gas atoms become excited when hit by these charged particles and release visible light. Each type of atom emits a specific color, resulting in a spectacular light display. The light display in the Northern Hemisphere is called an aurora borealis and in the Southern Hemisphere an aurora australis.

SPINNER

PURPOSE To demonstrate why the moon stays in orbit.

MATERIALS paper plate
scissors
marble

PROCEDURE

1. Cut the paper plate in half and use one side.

2. Place the marble on the cut edge of the plate.

3. Set the plate down on a table and slightly tilt it so that the marble moves quickly around the groove in the plate.

RESULTS The marble leaves the plate and moves in a straight line away from the paper plate.

WHY? Objects move in a straight path unless some force pushes or pulls on them. The marble moved in a circular path while on the plate because the paper continued to push the marble toward the center of the plate. As soon as the paper ended, the marble traveled in a straight line. The moon has a forward speed and, like the marble, would move off in a straight line if the gravitational pull toward Earth did not keep it in its circular path.

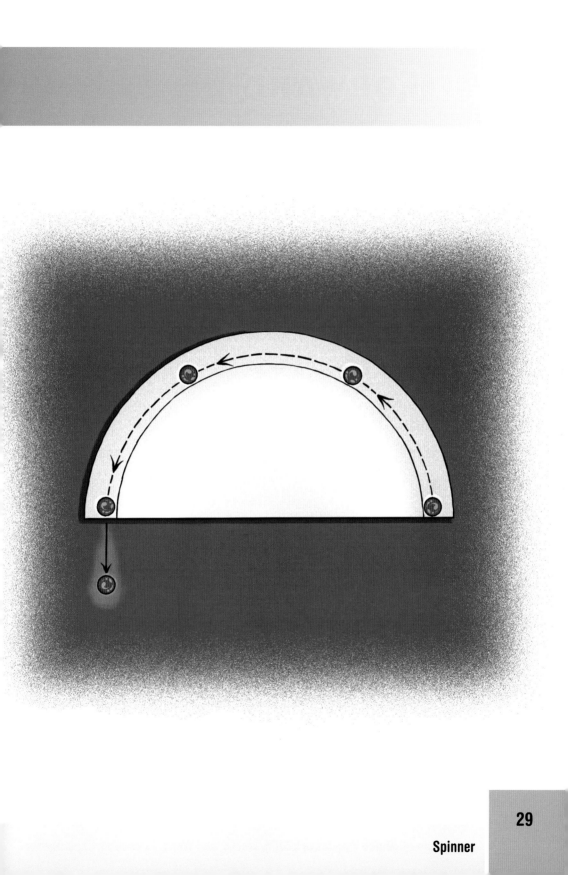

FACE FORWARD

PURPOSE To demonstrate that the moon rotates on its axis.

MATERIALS 2 sheets of paper
marker
masking tape

PROCEDURE

1. Draw a circle in the center of one sheet of paper.

2. Write the word EARTH in the center of the circle, and place the paper on the floor.

3. Mark a large X in the center of the second sheet of paper, and tape this paper to a wall.

4. Stand by the side of the paper on the floor and face the X on the wall.

5. Walk around Earth, but continue to face the X.

6. Turn so that you face the paper labeled EARTH.

7. Walk around Earth, but continue to face Earth.

RESULTS Facing the X-marked paper resulted in different parts of your body pointing toward the paper marked EARTH as you revolved around Earth. Continuing to face Earth allowed only your front side to point toward Earth during the revolution.

WHY? You had to turn your body slightly in order to continue to face Earth as you moved around it. In order for the same side of the moon to always face Earth, the moon also has to turn slowly on its axis as it moves around Earth. The moon rotates one complete turn on its own axis during the twenty-eight days its takes to revolve around Earth.

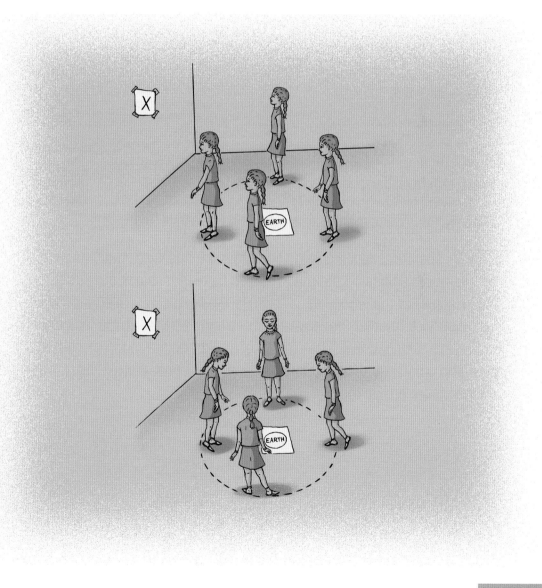

FACES

PURPOSE To determine the cause of the "man in the moon" image.

MATERIALS dominoes
table
flashlight

PROCEDURE

1. Stand six to eight dominoes on a table.

2. Darken the room and hold a flashlight at an angle about 12 in. (30 cm) from the dominoes.

RESULTS The dominoes form shadows on the table.

WHY? The dominoes block the light from the flashlight much as the mountainous regions on the moon, called highlands, block the sun's light. The shadows of the highlands fall across the flat plains, called maria. The highlands look brighter, as they reflect the light, and the maria look darker because of the shadows. The insides of craters on the moon also appear dark. The combination of highlands, maria, and craters forms the "man in the moon" pattern on the surface of the moon.

Star Clock

PURPOSE To determine why the stars seem to move in circles across the night sky.

MATERIALS umbrella—solid, dark color
white chalk

PROCEDURE

1. Use chalk to draw the stars in the Big Dipper on one of the panels inside the umbrella. Draw the entire constellation.

2. Hold the umbrella over your head.

3. Turn the handle slowly in a counterclockwise direction.

RESULTS The center of the umbrella stays in the same place, and the stars move around.

WHY? The stars in the constellation called the Big Dipper appear to move around a central star like hands on a backward clock. The stars make one complete turn every twenty-four hours, but unlike a clock, the hands are not in the same position each night at the same time. The stars reach a given position about four minutes earlier each night. Actually, the stars are not moving, we are. Earth makes one complete rotation every twenty-four hours, making the stars appear to move. The axis of Earth points to Polaris, the North Star, and it is this star that all the other stars appear to move around.

BIG DIPPER→

Star Clock

DAYTIME STARS

PURPOSE To demonstrate that the stars are always shining.

MATERIALS paper hole punch
index card
1 white letter envelope
flashlight

PROCEDURE

1. Cut seven or eight holes in the index card with the hole punch.

2. Insert the index card in the envelope.

3. In a well-lighted room, hold the envelope in front of you with the flashlight about 2 in. (5 cm) from the front of the envelope and over the index card.

4. Move the flashlight behind the envelope.

5. Hold the flashlight about 2 in. (5 cm) from the back of the envelope.

RESULTS The holes in the index card are not seen when the light shines on the front side of the envelope, but they are easily seen when the light comes from behind the envelope and toward you.

WHY? Light from the room passes through the holes in the card regardless of the position of the flashlight, but only when the surrounding area is darker than the light coming through the holes can they be seen. This is also true of stars. They shine during the daylight hours, but the sky is so bright from the sun's light that the starlight just blends in. Stars are most visible on a moonless night in areas away from city lights.

Daytime Stars

STREAKS

PURPOSE To determine why stars appear to rotate.

MATERIALS black construction paper
white chalk
scissors
pencil
ruler
masking tape

PROCEDURE

1. Cut a circle with a 6-in. (15-cm) diameter from the black paper.

2. Use chalk to randomly place ten small dots on the black circle.

3. Insert the point of the pencil through the center of the paper.

4. Use tape to secure the pencil to the underside of the paper circle.

5. Twirl the pencil back and forth between the palms of your hands.

RESULTS Rings of light appear on the spinning paper.

WHY? Your mind retains the image of the chalk dots as the paper spins, causing the paper to appear to have rings on it. A similar picture is produced when astronomers expose photographic plates under starlight for several hours. The light from the stars continuously affects the exposed film, producing streaks as if the stars were moving in a circular path. The truth is that the stars are relatively stationary and Earth is moving. The stars just appear to move around in the sky, but actually the film is moving with Earth as it spins on its axis.

Streaks

BOX PLANETARIUM

PURPOSE To demonstrate how planetariums produce images of the night sky.

MATERIALS shoe box
scissors
flashlight

black construction paper
cellophane tape
straight pin

PROCEDURE

1. Cut a square from the end of the shoe box.

2. At the other end of the box, cut a circle just large enough to insert the end of the flashlight.

3. Cover the square opening with a piece of black paper. Secure the paper to the box with tape.

4. Use the pin to make seven or eight holes in the black paper.

5. Point the shoe box toward a blank wall.

6. In a darkened room, turn on the flashlight.

7. Move back and forth from the wall to form clear images of small light spots on the wall. Make the holes in the black paper larger if the spots on the wall are too small.

RESULTS An enlarged pattern of the holes made in the paper is projected onto the wall.

WHY? As light beams shine through the tiny holes, they spread outward, producing larger circles of light on the wall. A planetarium presentation showing the entire night sky uses a round sphere with holes spaced in the positions of single stars and constellations. A constellation is a group of stars whose arrangement forms an imaginary figure. A bright light in the center of the sphere projects light spots on a curved ceiling, representing the sky. As the ball rotates, different star groups are seen. Because of Earth's revolution around the sun, different stars are viewed in the sky at different times of the year.

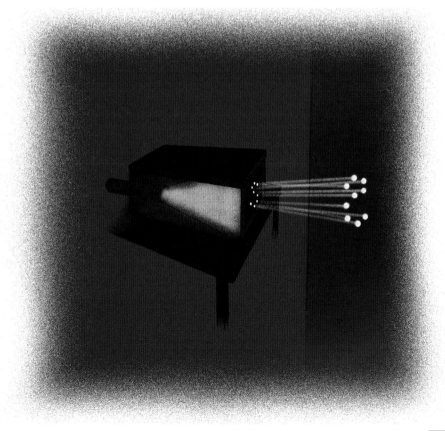

Box Planetarium

SPIRALS

PURPOSE To demonstrate the movement of a spiral galaxy.

MATERIALS jar, 1 qt. (1 liter)
1 sheet of notebook paper
paper hole punch
pencil

PROCEDURE

1. Fill the jar about three-fourths full with water.

2. Cut about twenty circles from the paper with the hole punch.

3. Sprinkle the paper circles on the surface of the water.

4. Quickly stir the water in a circular motion with a pencil.

5. View the water from the top and sides after you stop stirring.

RESULTS The paper circles swirl around, forming a spiral shape in the center.

WHY? The spinning paper only simulates the spiral movement and concentration of material of a star-studded spiral galaxy. Galaxies are thicker in the center; they actually bulge. The Milky Way galaxy is a spiral galaxy. It takes the Milky Way 250 million years to make one complete turn, but much space is covered during this rotation by the more than 200 billion stars. Our solar system is just a small part of this large spiraling mass that is 100,000 light years from edge to edge. A light year is a measure of distance, not time. One light year is the distance that light, traveling at a speed of 186,000 miles (300,000 km) per second, travels in one year.

INVERTED

PURPOSE To demonstrate how light travels through the lens of a refractive telescope.

MATERIALS 1 sheet dark construction paper
scissors
gooseneck desk lamp
masking tape
ruler
magnifying lens

PROCEDURE

1. Cut a paper circle from the dark paper to fit the opening of the lamp.

2. Cut an arrow design in the center of the paper circle.

3. Tape the circle over the lamp.

Caution: Be sure that the paper does not rest on the lightbulb. The bulb will get hot.

4. Place the lamp about 6 ft. (2 m) from a wall.

5. Turn the lamp on, and darken the rest of the room.

6. Hold the magnifying lens about 12 in. (30 cm) from the lamp.

7. Move the magnifying lens back and forth from the lamp until a clear image is projected on the wall.

RESULTS The image produced on the wall is turned upside down.

WHY? Light travels in a straight line, but when it hits the lens, it changes direction, causing the image to be upside down. Refractive telescopes have lenses similar to the one used in this experiment, and so stars viewed through a refractive telescope appear upside down.

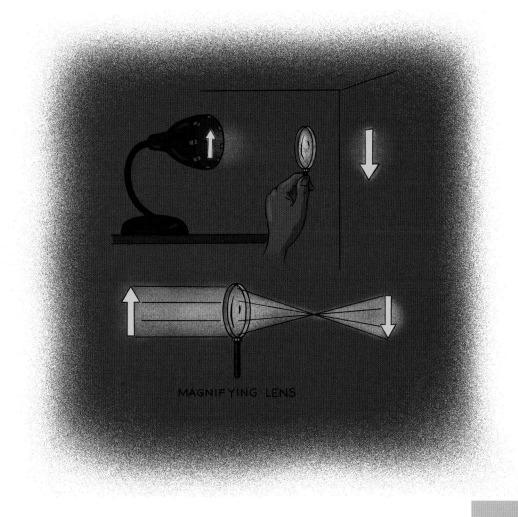

MAGNIFYING LENS

Inverted

SPACE BALANCE

PURPOSE To determine how mass can be measured in space.

MATERIALS hacksaw blade, 10 in. (25.5 cm)
4 coins, any size
masking tape

PROCEDURE

Caution: Have an adult cover the teeth of the blade with a strip of masking tape.

1. Tape the blade to the edge of a table.

2. Pull the free end of the blade back and release it.

3. Observe the speed at which the blade moves.

4. Use tape to attach two coins to the end of the blade, one on each side.

5. Pull the blade back as before and release it.

6. Attach two more coins to the blade and swing the blade as before.

RESULTS As more coins are added, the speed of the swinging blade decreases.

WHY? The swinging blade is called an inertia balance. Because the back-and-forth swing of the blade is the same in and out of a gravity field, the balance can be used as a measuring tool in space. Inertia is that property of matter by which it resists any sudden change in its state of motion or rest. As the mass of an object increases, the object's inertia increases. Therefore, it is more difficult to move a large mass.

You applied the same amount of energy to each swing, but as the mass increased, it took more energy to move it. The number of swings for a specific mass could be determined, and by counting the number of swings, the mass of an object can be calculated.

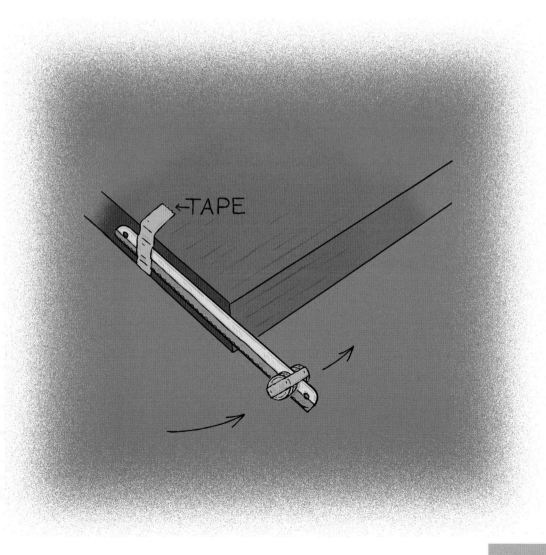

TAPE

RETROREFLECTOR

PURPOSE To determine how to measure the distance to the moon.

MATERIALS masking tape
2 flat mirrors
table
sheet of notebook paper
flashlight

PROCEDURE

Note: The experiment should be performed in a room that can be darkened.

1. Tape the edge of the mirrors together so that they open and close like a book.

2. Stand the mirrors on a table.

3. Tape the paper to the front of your shirt to form a screen.

4. Place the flashlight on the table so that the light strikes one of the mirrors at an angle.

5. Change the angle of the second mirror to find a position that reflects the light back to the screen on your shirt.

RESULTS A ring of light appears on the paper screen.

WHY? The light was reflected from one mirror to another before bouncing back to the paper screen. The retroreflector left on the moon was a set of mirrors similar to the ones in this experiment. The amount of time it took for a laser beam from Earth to reflect off the two and a

half feet square retroreflector was measured and the distance from
Earth to the moon calculated.

How High?

PURPOSE To determine how distance can be compared using an astrolabe.

MATERIALS

string
scissors
ruler
protractor

heavy bolt
drinking straw
masking tape
helper

PROCEDURE

1. Measure and cut a 12 in. (30 cm) piece of string.

2. Tie one end of the string to the center of the protractor and attach the bolt to the other end of the string.

3. Tape the straw along the top edge of the protractor.

4. Look through the straw (keeping one eye closed) at the tops of distant objects and have your helper determine the angle of the hanging string.

RESULTS The angle increases as the height of the objects increases.

WHY? To see the tops of the distant objects, the protractor had to be elevated. The hanging string remains perpendicular to the ground because gravity continues to pull it toward the center of Earth. As the protractor turns, the string has a different angle in relation to the straw. This instrument is called an astrolabe and can be used to compare the distances between stars, since the distance increases as the angle increases.

How High?

LIGHT METER

PURPOSE To demonstrate how to measure the brightness of light.

MATERIALS
yardstick (meter stick)
small box such as a shoe box
aluminum foil
wax paper

scissors
cellophane tape
tape
flashlight

PROCEDURE

1. Cut a large window in both ends of the box and two large windows in one side of the box.

2. Cover the openings with four layers of wax paper. Secure the paper with tape.

3. Fold a piece of aluminum so that it hangs in the center of the inside of the box, dividing the box. Secure the foil with tape.

4. Put the lid on.

5. In a darkened room, set the box on the floor and place the flashlight about 2 yd. (2 m) from the end of the box.

6. Observe the side windows.

7. Move the flashlight to 1 yd. (1 m) then ½ yd. (½ m) from the box's end.

RESULTS The side facing the light gets brighter as the light nears the box.

WHY? The aluminum foil reflects the light and the wax paper scatters it, causing the side facing the flashlight to be brighter. The brightness

52

increases as the light source nears the box. The box is an example of a photometer, an instrument used to measure the brightness of a light. A more sensitive photoelectric meter can be used to measure the brightness of light from stars. A star closer to Earth is much brighter than one of equal energy that is farther away.

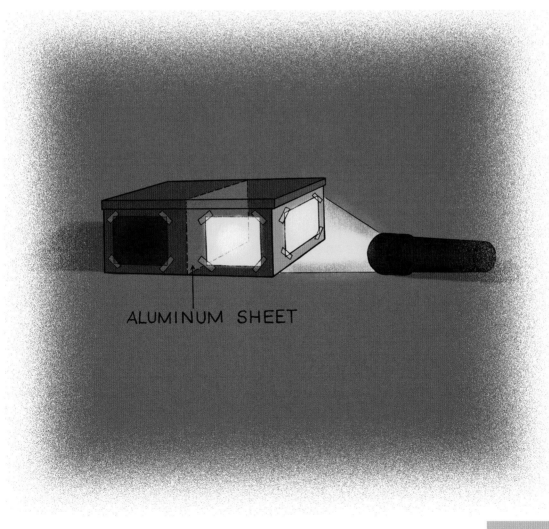

ALUMINUM SHEET

BOUNCER

PURPOSE To demonstrate how communication satellites work.

MATERIALS flat mirror
modeling clay
table

helper
flashlight

PROCEDURE

1. Use the clay to stand the mirror on a table positioned near an open door.

2. Have a person stand in the next room so that he or she can see the mirror, but not see you.

3. Shine the flashlight on the surface of the mirror.

4. You and your helper need to find a position that allows the light to reflect from the mirror so that your helper sees the light, but does not see you.

RESULTS The light beam is sent from one room and seen by a person in another room.

WHY? The shiny surface of the mirror reflects the light. Radio waves, like the light, can be reflected from smooth surfaces and directed to receivers at different places around the world. A signal sent to an orbiting satellite is bounced back at an angle to a receiver many miles away from the sender.

ATMOSPHERE The gases around a planet.

CONSTELLATION A group of stars that, viewed from Earth, form the outline of an object or figure.

CORE The center of something.

CORONA The outer surface of the sun.

DENSITY The scientific way of comparing the "heaviness" of materials.

GRAVITY The force that pulls toward the center of a celestial body, such as Earth.

HIGHLANDS Mountainous regions on the moon.

INERTIA Resistance to any sudden change in motion or rest.

MAGNETIC FORCE FIELD Area around a magnet in which the force of the magnet affects the movement of other magnetic objects; made up of invisible lines of magnetic force.

MAGNETOSPHERE The area affected by a magnetic field.

MARIA Flat plains on the moon.

PHOTOMETER An instrument that measures the brightness of a light.

Even More of Janice VanCleave's Wild, Wacky, and Weird Astronomy Experiments

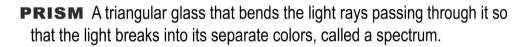

PRISM A triangular glass that bends the light rays passing through it so that the light breaks into its separate colors, called a spectrum.

REFRACT To bend.

SPECTRUM A range of values, such as the colors in white light.

VOLUME Space occupied by matter.

For More Information

American Astronomical Society (AAS)
  1667 K Street NW, Suite 800
  Washington, DC 20006
  (202) 328-2010
  Website: http://aas.org
  The AAS is the major organization of professional astronomers in North America. Locate an observatory near you, find out about Astronomy Ambassadors, and learn about the latest news in astronomy.

National Aeronautics and Space Administration (NASA)
  NASA Headquarters
  300 E Street SW, Suite 5R30
  Washington, DC 20546
  (202) 358-0001
  Website: http://www.nasa.gov
  NASA is the premier organization for all things space! Join the NASA Kids' Club, learn about the International Space Station and historic space missions, view solar system photographs, and learn more about space technology.

National Science Foundation (NSF)
  4201 Wilson Boulevard
  Arlington, VA 22230
  (703) 292-5111
  Website: http://www.nsf.gov
  The NSF is dedicated to science, engineering, and education. Learn how to be a Citizen Scientist, read about the latest scientific discoveries, and find out about the newest innovations in technology.

Royal Astronomical Society of Canada
203-4920 Dundas Street West
Toronto, ON M9A 1B7
Canada
Website: http://rasc.ca
The Royal Astronomical Society of Canada provides many educational resources, including Ask an Astronomer, observation calendars, photographs, and dates of public astronomy events.

Society for Science and the Public
Student Science
1719 N Street NW
Washington, DC 20036
(800) 552-4412
Website: http://student.societyforscience.org
The Society for Science and the Public presents science resources, such as science news for students, the latest updates on the Intel Science Talent Search and the Intel International Science and Engineering Fair, and information about cool jobs and doing science.

WEBSITES

Because of the changing nature of internet links, Rosen Publishing has developed an online list of websites related to the subject of this book. This site is updated regularly. Please use this link to access the list:

http://www.rosenlinks.com/JVCW/astro

Buczynski, Sandy. *Designing a Winning Science Fair Project*. Ann Arbor, MI: Cherry Lake Publishing, 2014.

Ford, Adam. *Stars: A Family Guide to the Night Sky*. Boston, MA: Roost Books, 2016.

Gardner, Robert. *A Kid's Book of Experiments with Stars*. New York, NY: Enslow Publishing, 2016.

Gifford, Clive. *Astronomy, Astronauts, and Space Exploration*. New York, NY: Crabtree Publishing, 2016.

Greve, Tom. *Astronomers*. North Mankato, MN: Rourke Educational Media, 2016.

Kawa, Katie. *Freaky Space Stories*. New York, NY: Gareth Stevens Publishing, 2016.

Kruesi, Liz. *Space Exploration*. Minneapolis, MN: ABDO Publishing, 2016.

Kuskowski, Alex. *Stargazing*. Minneapolis, MN: Super Sandcastle, 2016.

McGill, Jordan. *Space Science Fair Projects*. New York, NY: AV2 by Weigl, 2012.

Nichols, Michelle. *Astronomy Lab for Kids: 52 Family-Friendly Activities*. Beverly, MA: Quarry Books, 2016.

Riggs, Kate. *Moons*. Mankato, MN: Creative Education/Creative Paperbacks, 2015.

Rockett, Paul. *70 Thousand Million, Million, Million Stars in Space*.

Chicago, IL: Capstone Raintree, 2016.

Saucier, C. A. P. *Explore the Cosmos Like Neil DeGrasse Tyson: A Space Science Journey.* Amherst, NY: Prometheus Books, 2015.

Spilsbury, Louise. *Space.* New York, NY: PowerKids Press, 2015.

Wittekind, Erika. *Benjamin Banneker: Brilliant Surveyor, Mathematician, and Astronomer.* Minneapolis, MN: ABDO Publishing, 2016.

INDEX

A

astrolabe, 50
astronomy, explanation of, 4
atmosphere, 19, 27
aurora australis, 27
aurora borealis, 27

B

Big Dipper, 34

C

centripetal force, 13
constellations, 34, 41
core of the sun, 23
corona of the sun, 14
craters on the moon, 32

D

density, 23

E

Earth, 11, 13, 26–27, 28, 30–31, 38,
    50, 53
    atmosphere of, 19, 27
    measuring distance to the
      moon, 49
    revolution around the sun, 41
    rotation of, 34, 38
    and solar winds, 16–17

G

galaxies, 4, 42
gravity, 28, 46, 50
    and planetary paths, 9
    and satellites, 11, 13
    of the sun, 9, 23

H

highlands of the moon, 32

I

inertia, 46
inertia balance, 46
International Space Station, 4

L

light, 14, 19, 21, 27, 32, 41, 45,
    48–49, 54
    measuring brightness of,
      52–53
    separating colors of, 25
    from stars, 36, 38
light year, 42–43

M

magnetic force field, 16
magnetosphere, 16, 17, 26
maria of the moon, 32
mass, 23, 46–47

Even More of Janice VanCleave's Wild, Wacky, and Weird Astronomy Experiments